DRUGS & CONSEQUENCES

THE TRUTH ABOUT
OXYCODONE
AND OTHER
NARCOTICS

KRISTI LEW

ROSEN
PUBLISHING®

New York

Published in 2014 by The Rosen Publishing Group, Inc.
29 East 21st Street, New York, NY 10010

Copyright © 2014 by The Rosen Publishing Group, Inc.

First Edition

Library of Congress Cataloging-in-Publication Data

Lew, Kristi.
The truth about oxycodone and other narcotics/Kristi Lew. — First edition.
    pages cm. — (Drugs & consequences)
Includes bibliographical references and index.
ISBN 978-1-4777-1894-0 (library binding)
1. Oxycodone—Juvenile literature. 2. Oxycodone abuse—Juvenile literature.
3. Narcotics—Juvenile literature. I. Title.
RM666.O76.L48 2014
615.7'822—dc23

                                                                2013018133

Manufactured in the United States of America

CPSIA Compliance Information: Batch #W14YA: For further information, contact Rosen Publishing, New York, New
York, at 1-800-237-9932.

CONTENTS

Have you ever broken an arm or a leg? Or been injured while playing a sport? Even if you have not, you have most likely felt the pain of a headache or a sore throat at some point during your lifetime. Now imagine having that kind of pain and magnifying it until it hurts so much that you can barely think of anything else. According to a 2011 study conducted by the Institute of Medicine, more than one hundred million Americans suffer from this type of severe, chronic pain every year. Many others are injured in accidents or require major surgery, which can leave them in temporary, but excruciating, pain.

Some types of pain may be managed with anti-inflammatory pain relievers such as aspirin, ibuprofen, or naproxen (Aleve). Other types may respond to steroids, such as cortisol and prednisone, or acetaminophen (Tylenol). However, the acute pain of an injury or chronic pain that has proven untreatable by other means often requires stronger, prescription painkillers.

Oxycodone is the active ingredient in some of these painkillers, including OxyContin, Percocet, and Percodan. Although these drugs can be life-savers for the many people suffering from severe

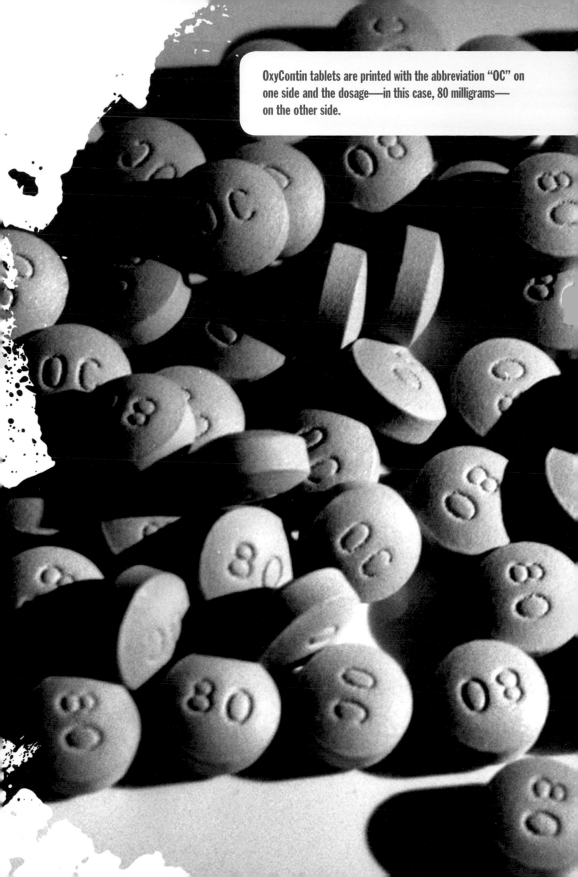

OxyContin tablets are printed with the abbreviation "OC" on one side and the dosage—in this case, 80 milligrams—on the other side.

pain, they have also proven to be extremely dangerous when taken irresponsibly.

How dangerous are they? According to a study conducted by the Centers for Disease Control and Prevention (CDC), 36,450 Americans died of a drug overdose in 2008. More than half of these overdoses were caused by the abuse of a prescription drug. Of the 20,044 prescription drug overdose deaths, nearly 74 percent were the result of the abuse of an opioid pain reliever such as oxycodone. In fact, prescription painkillers now cause more drug overdose deaths than heroin and cocaine combined.

You may think that you don't know anyone who has experimented with narcotics, but you might be surprised. Studies conducted by the Partnership at Drugfree.org indicate that as many as one in five teenagers has reported trying a prescription drug for the purpose of getting high. The studies also reveal that this experimentation occurs among those from all racial, ethnic, and socioeconomic backgrounds. In addition, data collected by the National Institute on Drug Abuse (NIDA) shows that prescription painkillers are one of the most commonly abused drugs by teens, after tobacco, alcohol, and marijuana.

It also appears as if new recreational users of prescription drugs are popping up every day. The latest data released by the National Survey on Drug Use and Health shows that, as of 2010, the number of people taking a prescription painkiller for nonmedical use for the first time was around two million. This number averages out to about 5,500 initiates per day. The only illicit drug taken by more people for the first time that year was marijuana. Of all the prescription drugs taken for non-medical reasons, painkillers were the drugs that were taken the most often.

Why would so many people experiment with prescription painkillers? New users of prescription drugs often report that they perceive these drugs to be less dangerous than illegal street drugs. Sadly, what they are not aware of is that chemically, painkillers that contain oxycodone and related substances are very similar to heroin—and they are just as deadly.

CHAPTER 1

Feeling No Pain

Oxycodone and other prescription painkillers are narcotic drugs. The word "narcotic" comes from the Greek word meaning "stupor." When taken in moderation, these drugs dull the senses, relieve pain, and promote sleep. They can also produce a profound sense of euphoria, or well-being. In high doses, however, narcotics can cause troubled breathing, coma, and death.

In general society, the term "narcotic" is sometimes used to mean any type of illicit drug, whether it actually produces

Opiates are derived from the milky sap of the opium poppy's seedpod.

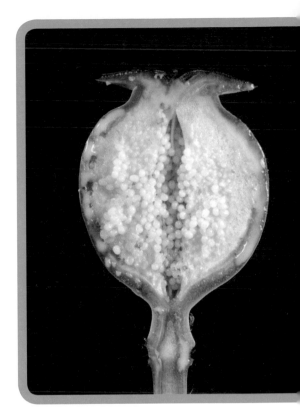

narcotic effects or not. But in the law enforcement and medical communities, the word "narcotic" is reserved for drugs related to the opiate family, including opium, opium derivatives, and their synthetic (meaning that they are made artificially by humans) or semi-synthetic counterparts.

Opiates

Some narcotics, such as opium, morphine, and codeine, are naturally occurring substances called opiates. Opiates are found in the milky sap of the seedpods of a particular type of poppy plant, called the opium poppy. The opium poppy's scientific name is *Papaver somniferum*. There are more than seven hundred species of poppy plants in the family *Papaveraceae*, but not all of them contain opium. Some, such as the California poppy and the snow poppy, are prized for their ornamental properties, not their narcotic potential.

The opium poppy grows best in warm, dry climates and is native to Turkey. According to a report by PBS's *Frontline*, a vast majority of opium poppy cultivation today takes place in a narrow, mountainous region that stretches from Turkey through Iran, Afghanistan, and Pakistan. The plant is also commonly grown in Poland, the Netherlands, the Czech Republic, Romania, India, and Canada.

The opium poppy plant is an annual, meaning that it lives and flowers for a single growing season. Its growth cycle lasts approximately 120 days. About ninety days after a poppy seed is planted, a poppy flower is formed. The flower petals fall away after a few days and a seedpod is left behind. During the next ten to twelve days, the seedpod ripens and grows to about the size of an egg. Opium is produced inside the seedpod during this ten-to twelve-day period.

Farmers extract the opium by cutting vertical strips in the seedpod with specially curved knifes and then scraping the sap off the seedpod as it oozes out. Exposed to the air, the opium turns from a milky liquid to a thick brownish-black gum. Farmers bundle the gummy mass into bricks or balls that are sold on the black market.

Opioids

Drugs manufactured to have narcotic effects on the body are called opioids. Some opioids are semisynthetic, meaning that they are manufactured by changing the chemical structure of opium. Semisynthetic opiate derivatives include heroin, OxyContin, Percocet, Percodan, Vicodin, Dilaudid, and Lortab. Other opioids are fully synthetic chemical compounds

Oxycodone is a semisynthetic opiate derivative of codeine. The painkiller Percodan is a mixture of oxycodone and aspirin.

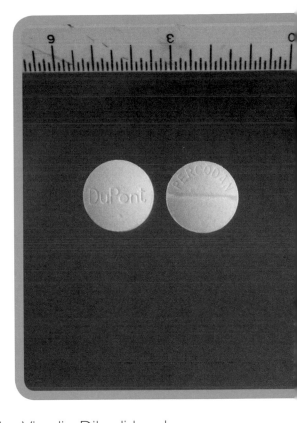

manufactured in laboratories to mimic the effects of an opiate on the body. Fully synthetic opi-oids include Demerol, Darvan, and methadone.

OxyContin, Percocet, and Percodan belong to a class of chemicals called oxycodone. Vicodin, Dilaudid, and Lortab are slightly different in their chemical makeup and are hydrocodones. Both classes of chemicals are derived from codeine.

OxyContin, Percocet, Percodan, Vicodin, Dilaudid, and Lortab are registered trade names for specific medications manufactured by different pharmaceutical companies. Narcotics also go by a variety of street names. Popular names for OxyContin include "hillbilly heroin," "OC," "oxy," "oxycot-ton," or just "cotton." Vicodin pills are often called "vikes," and Percocet tablets have been nicknamed "percs." The term "happy pills" may be applied to any number of narcotic pre-scription painkillers. Heroin is also an opiate. It is known on the street as "brown sugar," "junk," "smack," and a variety of other nicknames.

A Short History of Narcotics

In the early 1800s, pharmacists discovered that most of opium's painkilling powers come from a substance that it contains: morphine. Named for Morpheus, the Greek god of sleep, morphine soon became the favored painkiller for medical applications. Unfortunately, the drug also turned out to be highly addictive.

In 1898, a German scientist, working for the Bayer pharmaceutical corporation, discovered a compound that had nearly the same pain-reliving properties of morphine without, he believed, the side effect of addiction. Bayer used the compound in a potent cough suppressant and named it heroin. Over the next several years, culminating in 1902, medical journals seriously discussed the use of heroin as a possible cure for morphine addiction. As a result, heroin addiction skyrocketed the following year.

Like morphine, the chemical that serves as the starting material for the production of oxycodone is isolated from opium. German scientists first manufactured oxycodone in 1916. It was promoted as a nonaddictive replacement for narcotics such as heroin, which had been banned as an over-the-counter (OTC) drug by the Harrison Narcotic Act of 1914. The Harrison Narcotic Act made it illegal for anyone other than a doctor or pharmacist to sell large doses of opiates.

Oxycodone was first introduced in the United States in 1939, but it did not become widely known until it was

In the early 1800s, German pharmacist Friedrich Wilhelm Sertürner discovered a way to isolate morphine from opium.

released under the trade name Percodan in the 1950s. By 1963, California's attorney general declared that the drug accounted for at least one-third of drug addicts in the state.

In response to the growing problem of drug addiction, President Richard Nixon proposed and the U.S. Congress passed into law the Comprehensive Drug Abuse Prevention and Control Act of 1970. This law requires pharmaceutical companies to strictly monitor the physical safety and distribution of certain drugs. Under this act, drugs are divided into five classes, or schedules, depending on their potential for abuse, medical usefulness, and safety. Schedule I drugs have the highest potential for abuse, no commonly accepted medical use, and an unreliable safety record. Heroin, LSD, and marijuana are a few Schedule I controlled substances.

Schedule II substances are slightly less addictive than Schedule I substances. Morphine, opium, and codeine are

PILL MILLS

"Pill mill" is a term used by police investigators to describe a doctor, clinic, or pharmacy that prescribes or distributes prescription medication inappropriately. It is against federal regulations for a doctor to prescribe medication without a valid medical reason. If it is deemed that a doctor is doing so, he or she can be charged with drug trafficking, a felony that carries the possible penalty of life in prison.

According to a *CBS News* report, pill mills often advertise themselves as independent pain management centers. They often require no medical records, perform a minimal physical exam (if any), and accept only cash. To avoid detection, these centers tend to open, close, and reappear in a different location quickly. Although pill mills exist all over the country, the U.S. Drug Enforcement Administration (DEA) believes that a large majority of them are operated in Florida and Texas.

Florida's governor Rick Scott signed a bill into law that is designed to make it harder for pill mills to operate in that state.

Schedule II narcotics, as are OxyContin, Percocet, and Demerol. Vicodin and Tylenol with codeine are classified as Schedule III substances because they contain fewer opioid active ingredients per dosage.

OxyContin

Purdue Pharma released OxyContin in 1996. The drug was formulated to provide pain relief over a twelve-hour period. In comparison, other narcotics had to be administered about every four hours. The time-release formula found in OxyContin finally allowed patients in severe pain to get a full night's rest.

The drug quickly became a favorite with sufferers of intractable, or untreatable, chronic pain and their doctors. Not only did it last longer but, unlike other oxycodone-containing drugs like Percodan and Percocet, which are cut with aspirin and acetaminophen, respectively, OxyContin is pure, uncut oxycodone. The long-term use of aspirin and acetaminophen can cause liver damage, a concern that users of OxyContin and their doctors did not have to worry about.

In addition, many doctors perceived OxyContin as having less potential for abuse than other narcotics, a view that pharmaceutical sales representatives and the original U.S. Food and Drug Administration (FDA) labeling may have perpetuated, or maintained. In its original FDA filing for drug approval, the pharmaceutical company classified the drug's potential for abuse as low because of its time-release formula. The FDA allowed the pharmaceutical company to state that the formulation may reduce the risk of abuse on the drug's label. Purdue Pharma officials speculated that addicts would not be interested in OxyContin because of its time-release formula, preferring instead to use substances that would give them an immediate high. What these officials failed to appreciate was an addict's ability to work around the time-release formulation and release the drug's power all at one time.

In what the FDA now categorizes as an "aggressive" marketing campaign, Purdue Pharma sales representatives targeted primary care physicians and, at times, may have indicated that the drug should be used for chronic pain before all other options were exhausted. As a result, some doctors began to prescribe the drug exclusively for their chronic pain–suffering patients, as well as for more short-term ailments such as pain from a fall or a sports injury, greatly increasing the availability of the drug to potential abusers. In July 2001, the FDA required Purdue Pharma to change the labeling of OxyContin to include a "black box" warning. This labeling is the FDA's strongest warning for an approved substance and cautions the user of the lethal, or deadly, consequences of taking the drug in an unapproved manner.

2

Flooding the Brain

When opiate painkillers are used under a doctor's care, they are generally safe and effective. Misuse and abuse of these drugs, however, can easily turn deadly. According to a study performed by the CDC, overdose deaths due to the misuse of narcotic painkillers have more than tripled since 2001. The director of the CDC, Dr. Thomas Frieden, has characterized this abuse as a problem of "epidemic" proportions.

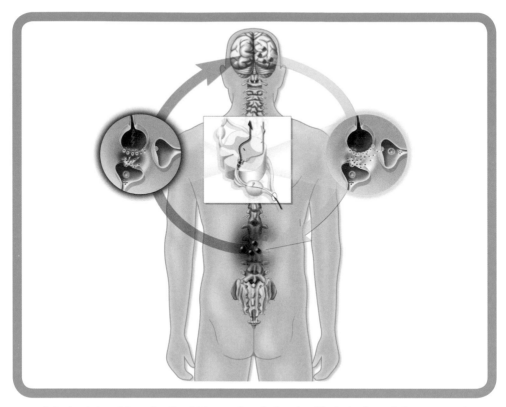

Pain signals travel from the site of injury to the spinal cord and brain (*red arrow*). In response, the brain sends a signal back ordering the release of endorphins (*blue arrow*).

The Effects of Narcotics on the Body

Opioid painkillers work by mimicking the body's natural pain-relieving chemicals. When a part of the body perceives pain, an electrical signal, called a nerve impulse, travels down a neuron, or nerve cell, to the spinal cord or brain. A signal is sent back that orders the release of chemicals called endorphins. The endorphins travel to special receptor cells in the spinal cord, brain, or other parts of the body. When the endorphins interact with these receptors, they block the perception of the pain. The underlying cause of the pain is still there, but the sense of pain is dulled.

Opiates and opioids interact with these receptors in the same way that endorphins do. In fact, scientists discovered the receptors while studying the ways in which narcotics, such as heroin and morphine, affect the brain. The only logical explanation for the existence of these receptors in the body was that the body had its own opiate-like substances. The word "endorphin" is a shortened version of the term "endogenous morphine." "Endogenous" is a term applied to a substance or process that is produced within or originates from the body.

Once an endorphin attaches to an opioid receptor, the perception of pain lessens. Nevertheless, chemicals called enzymes almost immediately break the connection between endorphin and receptor. The endorphin molecule is released unchanged, allowing it to be recycled and reused by the body. Opiates and opioids introduced into the body are resistant to these enzymes and stay in the receptor longer, prolonging pain relief.

Although pain and stress are the primary triggers for the release of endorphins, exercise, meditation, acupuncture, massage therapy, and even eating red-hot chili peppers can also trigger their release. The feelings of pleasure and satisfaction that some people feel after a prolonged exercise session is often called a "runner's high." The natural endorphins produced by the body are not normally considered addictive, but some

people may become addicted to this feeling of well-being, caus-
ing them to exercise excessively or inflict pain on themselves
in order to feel that rush. Scientists have also discovered that
some types of depression are linked to decreased endorphin
production.

The Effects of Narcotics on the Brain

Endorphins are released by the pituitary gland in response to
signals from a part of the brain called the hypothalamus. Every
person's body produces varying amounts of endorphins. Given
the same stimuli, different people may also report radically
different perceptions of pain. Unfortunately, doctors have no
scientific way of accurately measuring the pain a person feels.
They most often rely on patients grading their pain level on a
scale of one to ten.

When people are prescribed narcotics for pain relief and
use them as directed, the medication does not normally produce an overwhelming feeling of euphoria. All the narcotic does
is ease pain. If prescription painkillers do have that elated effect,
their dosage may need to be adjusted by a doctor, as these
feelings can increase the risk of addiction.

Continued use of narcotics can alter the chemistry of the
brain, decreasing the amount of natural endorphins that are
released. Narcotics have an immediate effect on the body.
Endorphins cannot work quite that quickly. Even while under
a doctor's care, use of an opioid can result in physical dependence on the drug. Someone physically dependent on opioids

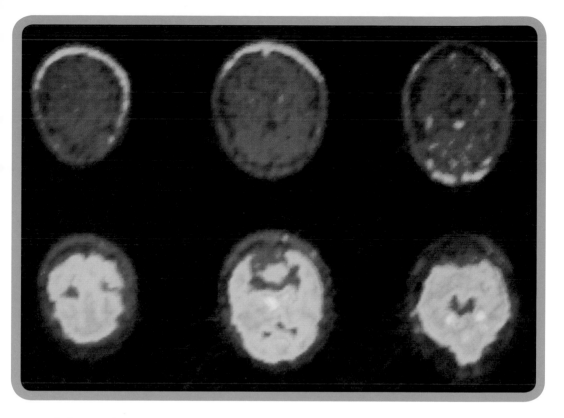

Brain scans of people who use opiate-like drugs show changes in their brain activity, which can sometimes be permanent.

will go through withdrawal symptoms if he or she stops taking them because the body cannot release endorphins in large enough quantities fast enough to mimic the effects of the drug.

The longer someone uses a narcotic, the more likely his or her body will develop a tolerance to the drug. The more tolerant the body gets, the higher the dosage the person has to take to get the same effect. This is the reason why taking someone else's pain medication is so dangerous. Someone who has been dealing with chronic pain from an injury or terminal cancer has built up a tolerance for these drugs over time. If someone who does not have chronic pain takes one of these drugs, it can flood the brain and easily lead to an overdose.

Withdrawal

Someone who is physically dependent on or is abusing opioids will likely experience withdrawal symptoms when he or she stops taking the drug. Early withdrawal symptoms include watery eyes, runny nose, and sweating. Symptoms generally progress to restlessness, irritability, muscle and bone pain, nausea, vomiting, diarrhea, tremors, alternating chills and flushes with excessive sweating, increased heart rate and blood pressure, severe depression, and an overwhelming craving for the drug.

Depending on the particular opioid drug, these symptoms may last a few days or weeks. Doctors can lessen and some-times prevent the symptoms of withdrawal by tapering down the dosage of the medication and weaning a patient off the drug gradually.

Withdrawal from opioids can cause major depression. A medical professional needs to manage a patient's withdrawal because the symptoms can be difficult physically and emotionally.

THE TEEN BRAIN

Using new technologies, such as magnetic resonance imaging (MRI), scientists have learned a lot about the human brain over the last decade. One thing they have determined is that the teenage brain undergoes massive change during adolescence. Using drugs during this period of development may well change brain chemistry for good.

According to experts involved with the Partnership at Drugfree .org, most addictions begin in adolescence, possibly because the brain matures from the back to the front. The cerebellum, which scientists are beginning to think has an effect on regulating pleasure and fear responses, is at the back of the brain and is one of the first areas to mature. The prefrontal cortex, on the other hand, is in the front of the brain and is one of the last regions to mature. The prefrontal cortex controls reasoning, behavior, urges, and impulses. The differences in the maturation of different areas of the brain could make teenagers more vulnerable to drug addiction.

Side Effects

Most drugs have unintended side effects, and prescription painkillers are no exception. Oxycodone may cause an allergic reaction in some people. Symptoms to watch out for include itching or hives, swelling in the hands, swelling or tingling of the face or throat, tightness in the chest, and difficulty breathing. Anyone who has ever had an allergic reaction to codeine, hydrocodone, dihydrocodeine, morphine, Tylox, or Vicodin should not take pain relievers containing oxycodone.

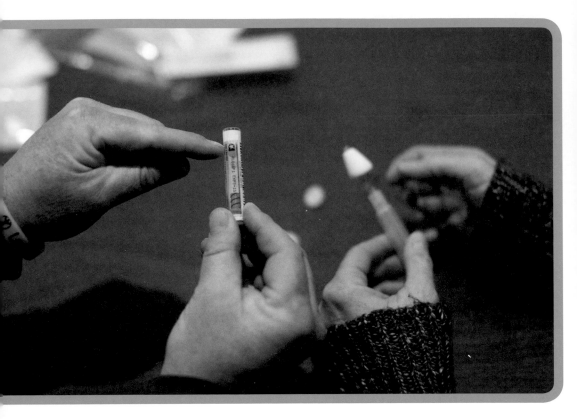

Overdose is a major risk when people use narcotics inappropriately. Some communities have trained volunteers who are likely to encounter an opioid overdose to administer blockers, such as the naloxone nasal spray seen here, that can counteract the effects of the drugs.

Opioid medications may also cause irregular heartbeat, dizziness, drowsiness, fainting, vomiting, severe constipation, sweating, and cold and clammy skin.

Narcotics are central nervous system depressants. They often cause drowsiness, impaired judgment, and an inability to concentrate. They can also slow or stop breathing, leading to loss of consciousness, coma, or death. People with asthma are especially at risk of deadly complications. Operating a vehicle while under the influence of a narcotic can be deadly due to impaired reflexes or loss of consciousness.

According to the National Institute on Drug Abuse, the abuse of prescription opioids causes more overdose deaths than the abuse of any other drug, including heroin and cocaine. A study conducted by the CDC in 2011 shows that more than forty people die every day because of an overdose of a prescription painkiller. Combining these drugs with alcohol and medications, such as antihistamines, barbiturates (Seconal or other sleeping pills), or benzodiazepines (Xanax or Valium), which are also central nervous system depressants, can increase the likelihood of life-threatening breathing complications. Symptoms of an overdose include constricted pupils, cold and clammy skin, confusion, seizures, extreme drowsiness, and slowed breathing. If you or a friend have taken a painkiller containing oxycodone and develop any of these symptoms, get to a hospital immediately. Once there, be honest about what has been taken. Doctors may be able to administer a drug called naloxone, a short-acting opioid receptor blocker, which may be able to counteract the effects of the opioids if it is given within the proper timeframe.

MYTHS & FACTS

MYTH Only adults abuse prescription drugs.

FACT According to data collected by the National Institute on Drug Abuse, twelve- to seventeen-year-olds report the abuse of prescription drugs more often than the abuse of ecstasy, crack/cocaine, heroin, and methamphetamines combined.

MYTH Abusing prescription drugs is safer than abusing illegal drugs.

FACT Prescription drugs are intended to be used only as a doctor directs. If taken improperly, they can have dangerous short-term and long-term health effects, including death.

MYTH My friend took OxyContin and he is not addicted. I will not get addicted either.

FACT Drugs affect different people in different ways. You may not become addicted the first time you try OxyContin. Then again, you might not be as lucky as your friend was.

3

Hooked

L ike the perception of pain, the susceptibility to addiction differs from person to person. Scientists believe
the likelihood that an individual will become addicted
to a particular substance depends on a number of factors, including genetics, brain chemistry, and social environment.

Becoming an Addict

In an interview with *Shape* magazine, Dr. Russell Portenoy,
chairman of the Department of Pain Medicine at Beth Israel

Because their brains are still developing, teenagers may be more susceptible to drug addiction than adults.

Medical Center in New York City, stated that approximately 10 percent of the population has a genetic predisposition to addiction. People with family histories that involve alcohol or drug abuse may fall within this 10 percent. People struggling with depression, anxiety, or bipolar disorder are also particularly susceptible.

In addition, the NIDA points out that a person's age and stage of brain development may also be factors. Because the areas that regulate decision making, judgment, and self-control are still under development during the adolescent years, teens may be more prone to risky behavior, including drug experimentation. This behavior can have long-reaching effects because, although drug addiction can begin at any age, scientists have found that the earlier drug use starts, the more likely a person is to have serious drug abuse issues in the future.

How an opioid drug will affect the body depends on how much of the drug is taken, as well as the method in which it is introduced into the bloodstream. Previous exposure to the drug and others like it, as well as the user's expectations of what will happen, can also influence its effects. As natural endorphin production slows in the body of a person experimenting with narcotic painkillers, the more opioids he or she will need to prevent or relieve withdrawal symptoms, leading to physical dependence and addiction.

Experts define addiction as compulsive drug seeking and use even when the person exhibiting the behavior understands the negative consequences. Anyone taking more of an opioid drug than is prescribed, taking it more often, or taking it for reasons other than subduing pain is risking addiction. Someone who has tried to give up the drug but is drawn back to it because of strong cravings for it has already become addicted.

Pharming

The use of pharmaceutical drugs for nonmedical purposes is sometimes called pharming. A 2010 Substance Abuse and Mental Health Services Administration (SAMHSA) study found that more than 1.9 million Americans abused prescription painkillers in the twelve months prior to the study being conducted. The Partnership at Drugfree.org reports that nearly 70 percent of the teens that have abused prescription painkillers got the drugs from the medicine cabinets of friends or family. Teens also reported obtaining opioids from friends who were selling the

Drug experimentation during the teenage years can lead to drug abuse problems later in life.

"extra" pills they or a relative were prescribed to manage post-operative or other pain. Very few teens reported getting the prescription drugs they were taking from doctors, pharmacists, or the Internet.

Taking any prescription medication without the consent of a doctor is considered drug abuse. People abusing opioid drugs often take a higher dosage than is recommended. They may also circumvent the pharmaceutical company's time-release formula by crushing the pills, which they then snort, swallow, or inject into their bloodstream. The result is a major jolt of opiates hitting the body system all at one time, a practice that dramatically increases the risk of addiction and overdose.

The Cost of Addiction

The use of opioids can have devastating short- and long-term effects. Short-term effects include the risk of overdose and, consequently, death—especially if prescription painkillers are mixed with other substances, such as alcohol. Long-term issues include potential addiction as well as loss of self-esteem, problems with interpersonal relationships, and failure to learn coping skills to manage life without having to depend on drugs.

In addition, some addicts must spend an exorbitant amount of money to support their habit. An addict with a 560-milligram per day oxycodone habit, for example, would need to buy fourteen 40-mg pills to ease drug cravings. At pharmacy prices, which is about $6.80 per pill, that works out to be $95.20 each day. If the addict cannot obtain his or her painkillers from a pharmacy and is forced to buy the drugs on the street, he or she could be looking at spending as much as $40 per pill, or $560 per day.

Some addicts may eventually resort to selling prescription medications they have stolen in order to fund their own habit. The distribution or use of controlled substances for recreational purposes is illegal. The DEA calls this behavior diversion because the drugs are being redirected from their original purpose. Get

Selling "leftover" prescription medication is illegal. An arrest on drug charges can follow you well into your future.

caught and you can be arrested for dealing drugs, which can have far-reaching consequences for your future.

Other behaviors that can get addicts arrested include stealing prescription pads, forging doctors' signatures, and robbing pharmacies. The DEA reported that there were 686 armed robberies of pharmacies in 2010, an 81 percent increase over 2006. Some of these robberies turn deadly, too. In June 2011, David Laffer entered a Long Island, New York, drugstore, shot the pharmacist,

TRACKING POSSIBLE ABUSE

Prescription drug monitoring programs (PDMPs) track prescription drugs from doctor to patient to pharmacy. Currently, forty-one states have PDMPs in place and all but two—Missouri and New Hampshire—have passed legislation to institute the programs in the future. The purpose of these computer databases is to determine if a patient is doctor shopping (procuring prescriptions from multiple physicians) or pharmacy hopping (trying to fill the same prescription at multiple pharmacies). Both behaviors are signs of addiction or diversion. PDMPs may also be used to alert authorities to physicians who are prescribing pain pills inappropriately.

Nonetheless, there are problems with PDMPs. Some people are concerned about individual privacy when there is a government database tracking personal prescription information. Moreover, each state sets up its own database, makings sharing data problematic, if not impossible. As of February 2012, the *New York Times* reported that only twenty-four states have the ability to share their information with other states. In some states, such as New York, pharmacists may enter information into a PDMP, but they cannot access the information, making it nearly impossible for them to identify problem patients or doctors.

a seventeen-year-old clerk, and two customers before stealing hydrocodone. According to one news report, Laffer had amassed more than four hundred pills in the weeks before the shooting by filling six prescriptions from five different doctors. He was sentenced to life in prison without the possibility of parole in November 2011. In response to the increasing threat of violence, some pharmacists have begun to arm themselves.

Paying the Price

Physicians can be held liable for prescribing drugs inappropri-ately. In 2002, a court found Florida doctor James Graves guilty of manslaughter after four of his patients overdosed on OxyContin. According to the *New York Times*, Graves was the first doctor to be charged with manslaughter in such a case. He was sentenced to almost sixty-three years in jail. Graves maintains that his patients lied to him, saying they were in pain and that he did nothing wrong.

Unfortunately, people who are genuinely in pain have also paid the price for the high levels of prescription medication abuse. As doctors' prescription habits have been scrutinized more closely, more and more have become unwilling to pre-scribe opioid drugs even to the patients who really need them for fear of getting into trouble. This reluctance to prescribe the drugs can have a devastating effect on those who really are in excruciating, debilitating pain. In addition, these pain patients are looked on with suspicion if they seek relief by changing doctors.

Purdue Pharma has also faced lawsuits over OxyContin. In response, the pharmaceutical company implemented a ten-point program designed to thwart drug abusers that includes distributing tamper-resistant prescription pads to doctors, the production of public service announcements aimed at teens, and the development of monitoring programs to help prevent doctor shopping. In 2004, Purdue Pharma also started a pilot program in which some bottles of OxyContin were tagged

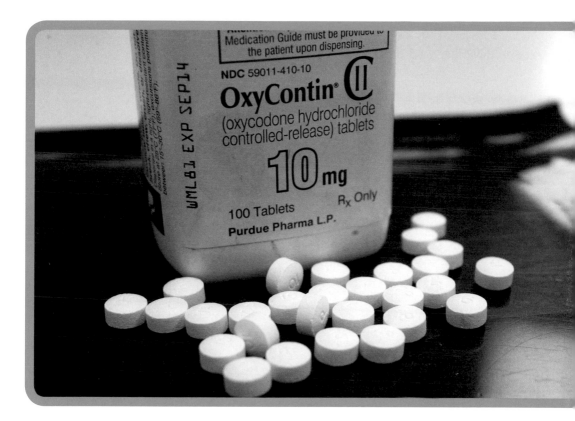

All OxyContin bottles are now equipped with RFID tags, allowing law enforcement officers to track stolen painkillers.

with radio frequency identification (RFID) tags. This tagging allowed the company, and the DEA, to accurately track the drug from the pharmaceutical plant where it is made to the pharmacy. If the bottles are stolen and later recovered in a suspect's possession, the DEA can track the bottles back to the pharmacy from which they were stolen, providing evidence to support its case. In 2007, Purdue Pharma began tagging all of its OxyContin bottles with RFID tags.

These tags not only help track bottles; they also provide proof of authenticity, preventing possible counterfeiting. Counterfeit drugs may not have oxycodone in them at all. Taking these drugs may be even more dangerous than taking pure oxycodone because users have no idea what drug they are actually taking.

Some experts speculate that the high rate of prescription drug addiction may also be fueling the rising cost of health care in the United States. As long as addicts can get these drugs through doctors and pharmacies, their habits are being subsidized by the health insurance system. Eventually, however, doctor-shopping addicts come up against resistance. With their legal source of pills cut off, they are often forced to turn to illegal means of getting the drug. With the high street value of opioid drugs, they soon run out of money and may turn to more illicit (unlawful), but cheaper, opioid drugs, such as heroin.

Getting
Unhooked

Treatment of a drug addiction can be as diverse as the reasons why people take drugs to begin with. Because someone addicted to opioids is likely to undergo a painful period of physical and psychological withdrawal symptoms, seeking professional medical treatment is not only advisable, but for many addicts absolutely necessary if they want to kick the addiction indefinitely.

Detoxification

Opioid drugs can change the chemical balance in the brain. As a result, withdrawal from an opiate can be extremely painful. Addicts often need help to rebalance those brain chemicals. Most people addicted to narcotics cannot stop on their own. The pain encountered when trying to wean themselves off opioid drugs sometimes allows addicts to convince themselves that they need to keep taking the drug as a legitimate painkiller. This is not a reasonable way to look at opioid addiction. Often, addicts are not capable of thinking clearly about their problems with drugs. In fact, friends and family members generally realize there is a problem long before the person taking the drug does. Detoxification programs in a medical setting can help with physical withdrawal symptoms and provide the assistance that people need to learn coping skills so that they will not feel the need to turn to drugs again in the future.

Treatment for oxycodone addiction may occur at an inpatient rehabilitation program, an outpatient treatment center, or a combination of both. Each of these options has advantages and disadvantages. Inpatient programs require addicts to remain at the facility until their treatment is completed. This residential requirement allows patients to go through the detoxification process in a safe environment and to receive the necessary counseling that will help them recover. It also removes the temptation and triggers that can cause a patient to seek out drugs and suffer a relapse. Outpatient programs

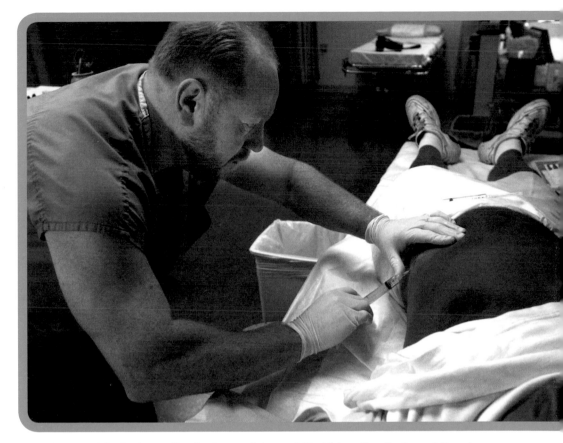

This doctor is implanting a pellet of naltrexone into an opioid addict months after he went through a detoxification procedure. The synthetic drug helps block the opiate receptors in the nervous system, preventing the patient from getting "high" if he uses an opioid in the following two months, when the possibility of a relapse is often the greatest.

allow addicts to return to their homes but require that they check in at the center to get medication and counseling on most days. Outpatient treatment is often recommended after leaving an inpatient rehabilitation facility.

Much of what is known about treating prescription painkiller addiction has come from the treatment of another narcotic:

heroin. In the 1960s, scientists discovered that methadone could be used in the treatment of heroin addiction. Methadone, a synthetic opioid painkiller, is still used to minimize withdrawal symptoms and reduce cravings for the drug. The use of methadone, which is administered daily by special clinics that are allowed to dispense the drug, greatly reduced the number of people injecting heroin. In turn, this decrease in intravenous (IV) drug use helped cut the number of new HIV/AIDS cases in half from 1993 to 2003, according to the National Institutes of Health (NIH).

Because methadone is also an opioid painkiller, it targets the same opioid receptors in the brain with which heroin, OxyContin, Vicodin, and other opioid drugs interact. However, its effects are less intense and longer lasting than the opioids that are commonly abused. Used in conjunction with other treatments, such as counseling, methadone maintenance doses have proved to be an effective treatment option for opioid addiction for nearly fifty years. A more recent synthetic opioid, called buprenorphine, generally has the same effects as methadone and is another treatment option.

Recovery

Methadone and buprenorphine are used to minimize the effects of physical withdrawal from an opioid drug. They do not address the underlying mental or emotional aspects of addiction. Therefore, these drugs are generally approved for use only in conjunction with other treatment options, such as counseling.

Counseling is an essential part of the recovery process. According to the FDA, weaning opioid addicts off the drugs without other types of treatment results in a high rate of relapse.

Once a person is stabilized and weaned off an opioid drug, another drug called an opioid receptor blocker may be used for a period of time in order to prevent a relapse. Naltrexone, the same drug used to minimize the effects of an opioid drug overdose, is one of those drugs. An opioid receptor blocker works by not allowing opioid drugs to attach to the receptors in the brain, eliminating the euphoric effects of the drug. Opioid receptor blockers should only be used by someone who has already stopped taking opioids. The FDA recommends that a person be opioid free for at least seven to ten days before a blocker is used, as they can cause severe withdrawal symptoms in someone who is still physically dependent or addicted to an opioid drug.

Some treatment centers offer what is called rapid detox, or anesthesia-assisted detox. During a rapid detox treatment, the patient still addicted to painkillers is put to sleep with a general anesthetic and given naltrexone. Because the patient is unconscious, he or she doesn't feel the withdrawal symptoms. Although this method can decrease the amount of time required for opioids to clear the system, studies have shown that this method is no better than other types of detox and, in fact, could be dangerous for some people in some situations.

If you are looking for help for a friend or for yourself, there are many combinations of treatment options. Try approaching a

Counseling is an important part of the recovery process. It can help recovering addicts learn how to cope with and avoid situations that may trigger their addiction.

family member, coach, or other trusted adult and ask this person to help you. Your doctor or the staff at your local hospital may be able to steer you in the right direction, too.

Tamper-Resistant Drugs

In May 2007, Purdue Fredrick, the parent company of Purdue Pharma, pled guilty to the misbranding of OxyContin and misleading regulators and doctors about its potential for addiction

THE FLOWER OF JOY

It is believed that the opium poppy was first cultivated in ancient Mesopotamia around 3400 BCE by the ancient Sumerians, who called it the "flower of joy." The Sumerians passed their knowledge of the plant on to the Assyrians. The Assyrians taught the Babylonians, who, in turn, passed their poppy-growing skills to the Egyptians. With each new civilization, the practice became more widespread.

In the 1300s, the Holy Inquisition was in full swing in Europe and the use of opium had been forbidden. Therefore, the mention of opium in historical records disappears for about two hundred years. In 1527, opium reappeared in the European medical literature as laudanum. Laudanum was a wildly popular "tonic" that contained opium dissolved in alcohol. It was prescribed for ailments as diverse as headaches to tuberculosis and even given to fussy infants to help them sleep. Unfortunately, some of those babies who were given the tonic never awoke.

and abuse. The courts decided that Purdue Fredrick's misbranding of the drug mislead doctors, who, in turn, prescribed the medication too freely, allowing too much of the drug into the market and making it easier for it to be diverted to illegal sources. The pharmaceutical company was ordered to pay $600 million in fines, one of the largest monetary settlements paid by a pharmaceutical company to resolve such a case.

In response to the criticism it received, the pharmaceutical manufacturer began work on reformulating OxyContin into a form that made it harder to abuse. In August 2010, the FDA approved a tamper-resistant formulation of OxyContin that deforms when it is crushed instead of turning to a fine powder as its predecessor did, making it much harder to snort or inject the drug. According to an article in the *New York Times,* the abuse of OxyContin appears to be on the decline. It is unclear if this abatement is the result of the new formulation or if it is in response to the reduction in the number of doctors pre-scribing OxyContin and, therefore, the drug's decreased availability on the street.

In April 2013, the patent for the original OxyContin formu-lation ran out, paving the way for generic drug manufacturers to introduce less expensive alternatives. Fearing a repeat of the problems caused by OxyContin, the FDA withdrew its approval for the original formulation, citing safety issues. This decision means that companies who wish to make a generic version of OxyContin must invent a way to produce a tamper-resistant pill without infringing on Purdue Pharma's patent for the new formulation. If they cannot make this type of pill, it is unlikely that consumers will see a cheaper, generic form of the painkiller on the market until Purdue Pharma's patent runs out in 2025.

TEN

1. Doesn't a person have to really want to get better for treatment to work?

2. Is a relapse a sign that an addict does not really want to stop using drugs?

3. How do I know if someone has a drug problem and how can I help?

4. Are some drugs more addictive and harmful than others?

5. How do I say no to drugs and still keep my friends?

6. Is it OK to take drugs in moderation?

7. Could I really get hooked the first time I try OxyContin?

8. I think I may be addicted to prescription painkillers. What are my treatment options?

9. What consequences do I face if I'm caught with prescription drugs that are not mine?

10. How are pharmaceutical companies, law enforcement agencies, and policy makers dealing with the prescription drug problem among young adults?

5

Making a Decision

Y ou may have heard the term "Gen X," meaning the generation of people born between the mid-1960s and the early 1980s. Most people call the following age group Generation Y, but their increasing reliance on and misuse and abuse of prescription drugs have lead some people to derisively call the generation born in the late 1980s to early 1990s Generation Rx instead.

Preventing Addiction

Different people have varying tolerances for different drugs. Whether you become addicted or not may be partially based on your genetic makeup and environment. Still, if you don't experiment with drugs in the first place, your chances of addiction decrease dramatically. If you do decide to try drugs, will you get addicted the first time you try them? It is hard to say. Scientists do not fully understand why some people become addicted while others do not. Nor do they know how much exposure to a drug is too much for a particular person. Most experts believe that trying drugs is a little like playing Russian

Florida teens read posters with pictures of young people at a Narcotics Overdose Prevention & Education (NOPE) candlelight vigil to honor those who died from drug overdoses. Every day, nearly one hundred Americans die of a drug overdose.

roulette. The first time may be the only time it takes. The more times you try, the more likely you are to develop a problem.

Teens may experiment with drugs for a variety of reasons. Some think that taking drugs makes them look cool. Some take them because their friends are taking them and they want to fit in. Others take drugs because they believe that the substances will help them control or manage their lives better. Sadly, this is generally not the case. In fact, taking drugs almost always has exactly the opposite effect. What people who abuse drugs perceive as "control" over their lives is actually an illusion created by the drug, not reality. Some people may abuse narcotics in an attempt to control academic, social, or emotional distress. Although this may work in the short term, the addiction that may ultimately take hold would only compound the problem.

HELPING A FRIEND OR FAMILY MEMBER

If you suspect that someone you know is misusing or abusing prescription painkillers or other narcotics, encourage him or her to speak to a parent, school guidance counselor, or other trusted adult. If you have a friend or family member who is recovering from drug abuse, there are several things you can do to help. For example, you could help the person avoid situations that could cause him or her to relapse, such as a party where you suspect there will be drugs. Maybe you could suggest that the two of you hang out together instead of going to the party.

Opioid drugs can be extremely helpful to people who need relief from short-term, excruciating, physical pain. They are never the answer for emotional distress. People who take these drugs for that purpose are setting themselves up for bigger problems.

Take a Stand

Before you are placed in a situation of having to turn down an offer of a narcotic or other type of drug, think about what you would say. Deciding how you will respond ahead of time can help prevent being caught by surprise. You don't have to make a big deal out of saying no. You also don't have to offer a reason for why you are saying no if you don't wish to give one. Just tell the person that you are not interested and leave it at that.

Another thing you might want to avoid is advertising that your mom, dad, or grandparent is taking a narcotic medication. Do not put yourself into a position of having someone you consider a friend try to influence you to steal medication from your family.

The majority of teenagers do not take drugs, so choose your friends wisely. If you are feeling like an outsider in your group, maybe it is time to look for a different group of friends. Try to find individuals who are enjoying life without the use of drugs. Join a theater group, get a couple of musicians or artists together, try out for a sports team, or volunteer in your community. If one of your former friends invites you to a party and you know there will be drugs there, make other plans. It is much

When asked at a high school assembly whether they could easily get prescription drugs, approximately half of a group of one thousand Kentucky teens indicated that they could get them without difficulty, if they wanted them.

easier not to put yourself into a position to have to say no. Above all, remember that it is your body and it is your decision about what you put into it.

Your Decision

You have many decisions to make in your life. Will you decide to experiment with drugs? Or will you decide that the pain, misery, and cost of addiction is too high a price to pay? Even if you are injured and a doctor prescribes a painkiller, you are still responsible for what you put into your body. If you are in pain, it is OK to take pain pills that are prescribed for you. It is also OK to not take them if you feel you don't need them. It is never OK, however, to take someone else's pain pills. These medications are designed to treat specific ailments in particular people. A pain pill prescribed for one person may not be the same as one prescribed for another. Doctors take into account the general health, age, and other considerations, such as interactions with other substances the person might be taking, into their

POPPY SEEDS AND DRUG TESTS

Do you like poppy seeds on your bagel or in your muffin? If your school or workplace does random drug testing, those poppy seeds could have you flagged as a heroin user. Opiates can be detected in urine for up to forty-eight hours after eating a poppy seed bagel or a slice of poppy seed cake. To combat the problem of false positives resulting from food that contains poppy seeds, the federal government raised the threshold from 300 nanograms per milliliter to 2,000 nanograms in 2005. Although eating a couple of bagels covered in poppy seeds could have tipped you over the old limit, you would need to eat three to four times that number of bagels to test positive with the new one. Claiming that a positive drug test is a result of the bagel you ate that morning will no longer hold up as an excuse. Taking cough syrup that contains codeine, though, will still push you over that limit.

decision on what is the best pain reliever for that particular person. Other people with different circumstances are placing themselves in danger by taking those pills. Remember that all medications have side effects. Some of those side effects might be mild, but some can be deadly.

If you decide to open the medicine cabinet and steal your parent's or grandparent's pills, you are not only potentially harming yourself, you are harming them. You are taking away their pain relief as well as their piece of mind. You're also taking away their trust in you. Trust is a very hard thing to win back. The only way to be certain that you never become addicted to opioid painkillers is never to try them to begin with. This is your life. The decisions you make matter.

GLOSSARY

acute pain Pain that is short-term, but severe.

chronic pain Less intense, but longer-lasting pain.

diversion The act of redirecting prescription drugs from their intended purpose.

doctor shopping Seeing multiple physicians for the purpose of getting prescription drugs.

endorphins The body's natural pain-relieving chemicals.

euphoria An intense sense of well-being.

initiate A person who tries something for the first time.

intractable Not easily controlled or relieved.

narcotic A drug that dulls the senses, relieves pain, and promotes sleep.

opioid A drug manufactured to have a narcotic effect on the body.

opioid receptors Special cells in the spinal cord, brain, or other parts of the body that interact with endorphins to block the perception of pain.

perception The identification and interpretation of information gathered by the senses.

pharmacy hopping Attempting to fill the same prescription at multiple pharmacies.

pill mill A doctor, clinic, or pharmacy that is prescribing or distributing prescription medication inappropriately.

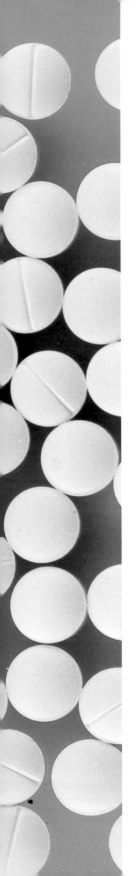

FOR MORE INFORMATION

Canadian Centre on Substance Abuse (CCSA)
75 Albert Street, Suite 500
Ottawa, ON KIP 5E7
Canada
(613) 235-4048
Web site: http://www.ccsa.ca
The CCSA is an organization dedicated to the
    reduction of alcohol and drug abuse–related
    issues through education, policy reform,
    and research. Its Web site provides tools and
    resources designed to support schools, com-
    munities, and families in the prevention of
    drug use by adolescents.

Drug Abuse Resistance Education (DARE)
9800 La Cienega Boulevard, Suite 401
Inglewood, CA 90301
(800) 223-DARE (3273)
Web site: http://www.dare.com
DARE provides a curriculum taught by trained
    police officers that is designed to educate
    young people about drugs and crime.

Narcotics Anonymous (NA)
P.O. Box 9999

Van Nuys, CA 91409

(818) 773-9999

Wcb site: http://www.na.org

NA offers a twelve-step program for recovering addicts that
includes regular group meetings and peer support.

National Institute on Drug Abuse (NIDA)

Office of Science Policy and Communications, Public
Information and Liaison Branch

6001 Executive Boulevard, Room 5213, MSC 9561

Bethesda, MD 20892-9561

(301) 443-1124

Web site: http://www.drugabuse.gov

NIDA offers educational materials, resources for people suffering from drug addiction and their families, and information
on the latest scientific research related to drug addiction
and its treatment.

The Partnership at Drugfree.org

352 Park Avenue South, 9th Floor

New York, NY 10010

(212) 922-1560

Web site: http://www.drugfree.org

The Partnership at Drugfree.org offers information on more
than forty commonly abused drugs, as well as material
that parents and caregivers need to educate young people
about the effects of drug and alcohol abuse.

Partnership for a Drug-Free Canada (PDFC)

Corus Quay

25 Dockside Drive

Toronto, ON M5A 0B5

Canada

(416) 479-6972

Web site: http://canadadrugfree.org

The PDFC provides information about commonly abused
drugs, as well as tips parents can use to talk to their adoles-
cents about drug use.

Substance Abuse and Mental Health Services Administration
(SAMHSA)

1 Choke Cherry Road

Rockville, MD 20857

(877) SAMHSA-7 (726-4727)

Web site: http://www.samhsa.gov

SAMHSA offers a treatment referral helpline, (800) 662-HELP
(4357), that can help callers find treatment facilities, support
groups, and other local organizations for their specific needs.

Web Sites

Due to the changing nature of Internet links, Rosen Publishing
has developed an online list of Web sites related to the subject
of this book. This site is updated regularly. Please use this link to
access the list:

http://www.rosenlinks.com/DAC/Oxyc

FOR FURTHER READING

Bjornlund, Lydia. *Oxycodone*. San Diego, CA:
Referencepoint Press, 2011.

Brequet, Amy. *Vicodin, OxyContin, and Other Pain
Relievers*. New York, NY: Chelsea House
Publishers, 2008.

Carlson, Dale, and Hannah Carlson. *Addition: The
Brain Disease*. Madison, CT: Bick Publishing
House, 2010.

Cobb, Allan. *Heroin*. New York, NY: Chelsea
House Publishers, 2009.

Colligan, L. H. *Drug Dependence*. New York, NY:
Benchmark Books, 2010.

Fisanick, Christina. *Addiction*. Detroit, MI:
Greenhaven Press, 2009.

Flint, Dirk. *Drug Crime*. Mankato, MN: Smart Apple
Media, 2011.

Kuhar, Michael. *Substance Abuse, Addiction,
and Treatment*. New York, NY: Marshall
Cavendish, 2011.

Mason, Paul. *Surviving Drug Addiction*. Mankato,
MN: Arcturus Publishing, 2010.

Medina, Sarah. *Know the Facts About Drugs*. New
York, NY: Rosen Publishing, 2010.

Newton, Michael. *Drug Enforcement
Administration*. New York, NY: Chelsea House
Publishers, 2011.

Olive, M. Foster. *Morphine*. New York, NY: Chelsea House Publishers, 2011.

Paris, Stephanie. *Straight Talk: Drugs and Alcohol*. Huntington Beach, CA: Teacher Created Materials, 2012.

Rooney, Anne. *Dealing with Drugs*. Mankato, MN: Amicus, 2011.

Sanna, E. J. *Heroin and Other Opioids: Poppies' Perilous Children*. Broomall, PA: Mason Crest Publishers, 2013.

Sayler, Mary Harwell. *Prescription Pain Relievers*. New York, NY: Chelsea House Publishers, 2011.

Snedden, Robert. *Understanding the Brain and the Nervous System*. New York, NY: Rosen Publishing, 2010.

Walker, Ida. *Addiction Treatment: Escaping the Trap*. Broomall, PA: Mason Crest Publishers, 2012.

Walker, Ida. *Painkillers: Prescription Dependency*. Broomall, PA: Mason Crest Publishers, 2012.

Wilkins, Jessica. *Street Pharma*. New York, NY: Crabtree Publishing, 2011.

Wolny, Philip. *Abusing Prescription Drugs*. New York, NY: Rosen Publishing, 2008.

BIBLIOGRAPHY

Centers for Disease Control and Prevention. "Vital Signs: Overdoses of Prescription Opioid Pain Relievers—United States, 1999–2008." November 4, 2011. Retrieved April 1, 2013 (http://www.cdc.gov/mmwr/preview/mmwr html/mm6043a4.htm?s_cid=mm6043a4_w).

Frontline. "Transforming Opium Poppies into Heroin." PBS. Retrieved February 18, 2013 (http://www.pbs.org/wgbh/pages/frontline/ shows/heroin/transform).

Goodnough, Abby, and Katie Zezima. "Drug Is Harder to Abuse, but Users Persevere." *New York Times*, June 15, 2011. Retrieved March 23, 2013 (http://www.nytimes.com/2011/06/16/ health/16oxy.html?_r=0).

Kelly, Kate. "The Accidental Addict: Got Back Pain or a Migraine? Read This Before You Pop a Painkiller." *Shape*, November 2011, p. 164.

Meier, Barry. "Doctor Guilty in 4 Deaths Tied to a Drug." *New York Times*, February 20, 2002. Retrieved April 3, 2013 (http://www.nytimes .com/2002/02/20/us/doctor-guilty-in-4-deaths- tied-to-a-drug.html).

Meier, Barry. "In Guilty Plea, OxyContin Maker to Pay $600 Million." *New York Times*, May 10, 2007. Retrieved April 3, 2013 (http://www.

nytimes.com/2007/05/10/business/11drug-web
.html?pagewanted=all&_r=1&).

Meier, Barry. *Pain Killer: A "Wonder" Drug's Trail of Addiction and
Death*. Emmaus, PA: Rodale, 2003.

National Institute on Drug Abuse. "DrugFacts: Understanding
Drug Abuse and Addiction." November 2011. Retrieved
March 21, 2013 (http://www.drugabuse.gov/publications/
drugfacts/understanding-drug-abuse-addiction).

Office of Diversion Control. "Controlled Substance Schedules."
Retrieved February 18, 2013 (http://www.deadiversion
.usdoj.gov/schedules/index.html).

Office of National Drug Control Policy. "Medication-Assisted
Treatment for Opioid Addiction." September 2012.
Retrieved March 23, 2013 (http://www.whitehouse.gov/
sites/default/files/ondcp/recovery/medication_assisted
_treatment_9-21-20121.pdf).

Pokrovnichka, Anjelina. "History of OxyContin: Labeling and
Risk Management Program." Federal Drug Administration,
November 13–14, 2008. Retrieved April 3, 2013 (http://
www.fda.gov/downloads/AdvisoryCommittees/Committees
MeetingMaterials/Drugs/AnestheticAndLifeSupportDrugs
AdvisoryCommittee/UCM248776.pdf).

Rehagen, Tony. "The Drugstore Drug War." *Men's Health*,
July–August 2012, p. 112.

RFID News. "Impinj and Purdue Pharma Inject RFID into Supply
Chain." February 12, 2007. Retrieved April 3, 2013 (http://

www.rfidnews.org/2007/02/12/impinj-and-purdue-pharma
-inject-rfid-into-supply-chain?tag=Health_Care).

Szalavitz, Maia. "Report: Chronic, Undertreated Pain Affects 116
Million Americans." *Time Online*, June 29, 2001. Retrieved
February 24, 2013 (http://healthland.time.com/2011/06/29).

Thomas, Katie, and Barry Meier. "Drug Makers Losing a Bid to Foil
Generic Painkillers." *New York Times*, January 2, 2013, p. B1.

U.S. Department of Health and Human Services. "Results
from the 2010 National Survey on Drug Use and Health:
Summary of National Findings." Retrieved April 3, 2013
(http://www.oas.samhsa.gov/NSDUH/2k10NSDUH/2k10
Results.htm#2.16).

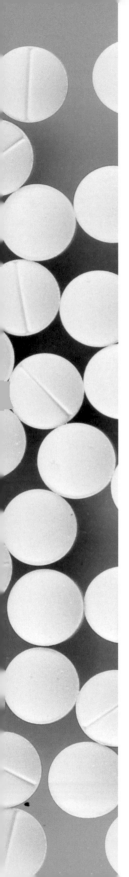

INDEX

About the Author

Kristi Lew has written more than forty books for teachers and young people. Fascinated with science from a young age, she studied biochemistry and genetics in college. Before becoming a full-time writer, she worked in genetics laboratories and taught high school science. When she is not writing, she can often be found sailing or kayaking around Tampa Bay or out on the back deck with her nose buried in a book.

Photo Credits

Cover, p. 1 Leonard Lessin/Photo Researchers/Getty Images; pp. 4–5 The Washington Post/Getty Images; pp. 8, 17, 27, 37, 46, 53, 54, 57, 59, 62 George Burba/Shutterstock.com; p. 9 Nigel Cattlin/Visuals Unlimited/Getty Images; p. 11 U.S. DEA; p. 13 Hulton Archive/Getty Images; p. 14 Joe Raedle/Getty Images; p. 18 JACOPIN/BSIP/SuperStock; p. 21 Hank Morgan/Science Source; pp. 22, 28 iStockphoto.com/Thinkstock; p. 24 Boston Globe/Getty Images; p. 30 Robert A. Pears/Photodisc/Getty Images; p. 32 Hill Street Studios/Blend Images/Getty Images; pp. 35, 39, 50 © AP Images; p. 42 © iStockphoto.com/clearstockconcepts; p. 47 © Douglas R. Clifford/Tampa Bay Times/ZUMA Press.

Designer: Sam Zavieh; Editor: Kathy Kuhtz Campbell; Photo Researcher: Karen Huang